WHEN HE *Whispers*

Verses of Inspiration and
Encouragement to Touch
the Heart and Uplift the Soul

Andrea L. Hines

FOREWORD BY PASTOR SHERYL BRADY

ISBN-13: 978-1-954818-04-0

Studio Griffin
A Publishing Company
Garner, North Carolina
www.studiogriffin.net

Cover Design by Ruth E. Griffin
Image by Lichtmeister/Shutterstock

Website: www.hiswords4u.com
Blog: www.hiswords4u.wordpress.com
Email: hiswords4u@bellsouth.net

Printed in U.S.A

Dedication

To the Past and the Future

For Godly parents --
The generational blessing of writing came from
my mother, Anna Wyles-Henson.
My father, Ernest Henson, was my best friend
and my greatest supporter.
While they have joined the cloud of witnesses,
I know they continue to peer over the balcony of heaven
to coach me through my journey.

For my grandchildren --
Christian and Jazzmen, you've blessed my life in
unimaginable, immeasurable ways.
Never be afraid to explore the possibilities.
Birth future generations
who will believe in God,
believe in themselves
and rise to heights yet unseen.

Foreword

In my years of Pastoral service at The River Church, I have been afforded the awesome opportunity of ministering to some of God's most precious children. However, few of them have become more precious to me than Sister Andrea Hines. I had no idea what God was giving me the day He made her a part of our church family. She has been a pillar in our house from day one!

Andrea is an extremely anointed writer. She came as a gift to us, and after all these years, we are still trying to understand the magnitude of the gift! I am humbled that God would trust such greatness into my hands.

When I think of her, words like, "dependable and devoted, faithful and firm, honest and honorable, tried, true, unswerving, and unwavering" are just a few of the words that come to my mind.

I can't tell you how many times her letters, cards, and even the simplest of notes have resuscitated my Spirit. Her simplicity allows her to make a profound human connection. When she writes, she reaches deep within herself causing the poetic to pour out of her like water escaping out of a broken vessel. Obviously, she has had her share of pain. Obviously, because of it, she has learned to tune her ear to the still small voice of God.

I understand that time is precious and priceless however, I encourage you to spend some of yours in the following pages. Find a sanctuary of solitude. Know that as you are refreshing yourself…God is rebuilding you. Will you join me in turning down the volume of life? If we listen close enough, we might just hear God "When He Whispers!"

Pastor Sheryl Brady
The Potter's House of North Dallas
Frisco, Texas

Author's Note

As I began to work diligently to select just the right poetic verses to be included in this first manuscript, I found myself doing what I have to do frequently. I took myself out of the equation, settled back, and asked God what He wanted to do. After all, the words are inspired by Him. The rhythm and style of the verses are of His choosing. The content is whatever He wants it to be: instructional, encouraging, loving, food for thought, etc.

I used to think God only spoke in a booming voice. I anticipated the earth would quake when He wanted to get my attention – you know, a "burning bush" experience. Instead, I find He loves to whisper to me in the quiet stillness of the early morning hours when it is just the two of us.

I began sharing our chats in 2004 through the website now named www.hiswords4u.com. Readers' comments that this book was a timely comfort or encouragement confirms God's timing is always perfect. He knows exactly what we need and when.

Since the first printing, "When He Whispers" has become a morning devotional, basis for bible study in prison ministry, included in workshops, and provided peace at the close of the day. As you read through it, you will notice there are no categories and nothing to guide you through the pages. I invite you to read the entries from cover to cover, or allow a title to catch your eye and ignite your curiosity. Either way, I pray the verses will speak to your heart. I pray you will be strengthened and encouraged by what you read. I pray your relationship with God will deepen as your hunger for Him increases. I pray this for you and more when He whispers…

Be blessed!

Acknowledgments

When you begin to name people in acknowledgments, you will always run the risk of forgetting someone or having hurt feelings by not mentioning your fourth cousin on your mother's side of the family. While that may be accurate, God has blessed me with a group of friends and associates who are secure in who they are and what their role has been in this drama called my life. That is just how good God has been to me. If they never see their names in print they know how much I love them and appreciate every physical and emotional seed they have planted in what is proving to be good ground. However, there are a few people I would like to introduce to you as I thank them for their contribution to *A's Accents* (the company introduced to share His expressions of creativity deposited in me) and the accomplishment of a dream deferred, but not denied. Named or unnamed, family, extended family, friends and enemies alike, it could not have happened without each of you.

Special thanks to:

Pastor Sheryl and Bishop Joby Brady
*For taking me to a place in my relationship
with God I did not know existed.*

Pastor Ronald Godbee
*Whose confidence in me continues to encourage me
and challenge me to explore the possibilities.*

My daughter, Audra
*Who has her own unique way of encouraging me
to believe in myself. I love you baby.*

Pastor Gloria Kennedy and Marylen Jennings
Longtime friends who know all of my secrets and love me still.

Connie Schwamberger
*My creative business partner
who has my eye for excellence.*

Francina Booker
My angel who is always faithful to pray.

Janet Campbell
Who has shared my journey in a very unique way.

Vee Garcia
Who showed me the power and value of the written word.

Lorraine Stephens
Who saw potential when I was still seeing problems.

Linda Cooks
First partaker of His whispers.

Al Richmond
Thank you for never giving up on me.

Tracy Mac
*Who let me know it is never too late
to make your dreams reality.*

None of this would be possible

if God had not chosen me to be His pen.

Father, how I love You!

CONTENTS

A Right Now God

"I'll get back to you later." Famous last words. Have you ever been in dire need of something, made your request and the response was, "I'll get back to you later?" You can understand a slight delay. The problem is, sometimes "later" never comes. You feel as if you've been placed on 'hold' indefinitely, ignored, or even worse, forgotten. Not with God. God is a right-now God. He is always working things out for you, and He is doing it right now. He is always guiding you. He's preparing you for some open doors, right now. You can talk to Him, now. He is with you as you read this "whisper," right now. You may not understand the things going on around you, but you are His priority right now. You may not even believe anything is happening. You feel at a standstill, but God is just closing a destiny delaying door right now. You may talk to Him and think you've been placed on permanent hold, but He is always, always, at work. As the CEO of heaven, God is the mover and shaker in your life and He's shifting something for you right now.

The manifestation may be later,
but God is indeed a right now God!
Praise the Lord... Praise the Lord... Praise the Lord!

A Tale of the Tongue

Lord have mercy, there I go running my mouth again.

Is it in the Word somewhere that talking too much is a sin?

I don't intend to do anything wrong.

I think I'm just having a chat

until I feel all of those daggers headed directly for my back.

To me it's really not meddling.

I mean everything for good.

So why can't I close my big fat mouth

like others wish that I would?

I guess there should be a law passed.

In my case, at the very least,

impose a ten thousand dollar fine

if my talking does not cease.

Lord, please help me keep silent;

or sweetly nod my big head;

or practice repeating over and over

"there's nothing more to be said."

Should I send a note of apology to everyone I know

just in case I've somehow offended them

and they may not have let it show?

God, I need you to help me.

I really don't know what to do.

I've got to conquer this "gift of gab"

if I'm going to be working for You.

I know that I have to remember

while You may want me to be bold,

there's no situation requiring my help

since You have it all under control.

I have no license to share my thoughts

when there's no invitation to speak,

or give my opinion, or anything else

my mouth has just sprung a leak.

I repent for any confusion.

I repent for hard feelings I've caused.

Perhaps if I'd put my tongue in reverse,

my mouth would have been forced to pause.

Lord, please let others forgive me and

please don't let them forget--

though my tongue is at times in rebellion,

God is not through with me yet!

Activating My Faith

In order to activate my faith, I must:

Forget my past (ALL those things which are behind me) and forget what other people say. They are not God in my life and only God's Word will come to pass. I must

Acknowledge Him as my Lord and Savior; my provider and my deliverer; my shield and my buckler; my present help in time of trouble; and God of the impossible. I must

Incline my ear to His voice; to His direction; to His commands; and to His guidance. It will not be sufficient for me to hear Him. I must then trust Him and obey. I must be forever

Thankful in everything – and I mean everything – not FOR it, but IN it. God has a plan for my life and whatever I do, whatever I go through is part of His divine design. I must then

Humble myself before Him and remember, regardless of what I have; regardless of what I am; regardless of what I ever hope to be; it's because of the lovingkindness, grace and mercy of an Almighty God.

Therefore, if things are rough, tight, trying and I think I have nothing left to stand on, that's the time for me to stand on the Rock and activate my faith.

An Invitation

I once received an intriguing piece of mail. On the outside of the envelope there was one word, *"Come"*. It wasn't very fancy, but there was something about this single word that let me know I was being invited to a very special occasion. I began to wonder about the reason for this event. Was someone being honored? How should I dress? Would anyone that I know be attending? Should I bring a gift for the host? Would there be refreshments, or should I bring my favorite culinary masterpiece? Suddenly I noticed I didn't actually see my name. Perhaps this wasn't even meant for me. I decided the best way to answer my questions was to open the envelope and see what was inside.

This is what I read:

"I bid you come. This event is being held in your honor. There is no "gift" required of you, but you should bring all of your cares, all of your worries, all of your burdens and be prepared to leave them. It doesn't matter what you decide to wear. When you enter in, you will be washed white as snow and receive a robe of righteousness with a matching garment of praise. If you were thinking of bringing a dish, do not be concerned. It is not a 'pot luck' affair. As a matter of fact,

don't bother to eat anything at all before you arrive. Come empty. A feast has been prepared for you with more than you could ever imagine. When you pull up to the table, you will never hunger and thirst again. There is no need for you to RSVP. This is a standing invitation. Whenever you decide to honor it, there will be room available for you. You see, everything you will ever need is enclosed: healing, deliverance, breakthroughs, provision, peace, protection, unconditional love… everything! By the way, don't worry about not seeing your name. It is already written in My guest book. If you received the invitation, it's because it was meant especially for you and I don't make mistakes. Join me won't you? I promise your life will never be the same. Love, Jesus "

I accepted the invitation. Then, as if all that I described wasn't enough, I received the greatest gift anyone could ever receive. The gift was salvation.

An invitation has been sent to each of you. Have you responded to yours? I certainly hope so. If not, today would be the perfect day.

…if thou shalt confess with thy mouth the Lord Jesus,
and shalt believe in thine heart that God hath raised him from the
dead, thou shalt be saved.

Romans 10:9

Are You Ready?

You've been jumping. You've been shouting.
You've been fasting and you pray.
Church on Sunday, Bible study,
quoting scriptures every day.
You've touched your neighbor three times.
You raise your hands. You bow.
You may have even shouted, "Money cometh to me now!"
You're expecting. You've been standing,
You just know you've passed each test.
Yet the things that you're believing for
don't seem to manifest.
Are you ready for abundance?
"Of course," you say, "I am!"
Can you really live in overflow?
"Try me, Lord. I can!"
As you're crying out to Him today
and seeking your breakthrough,
how have you handled blessings?
He's already given you?
Have you really been obedient?
Can He trust you all the time?
Does He always get the glory?
Is He always on your mind?

God says, "Before you query me
on why, why not, or when,
or feel a blessing
should have come to you and not to "them,"
be certain in the waiting time
you've really done your part.
Be certain of your motives.
I know what's in your heart."

Make sure He's your priority in all you say and do.
He's faithful and He'll give you
all the things He's planned for you.
Since He's God and knows what's best,
there are things He won't release
'til you're prepared for promise
and you're ready to receive.

Balance

As our lives become busier and more hectic every day, we
often wonder how we can ever keep things prioritized and
get everything accomplished. What we really need is to
find balance in the midst of it all:

Be prayerful as you seek God first in everything you do.

Allow time for yourself. You must take time for you.

Let go of the past because it only slows you down.

Always let an attitude of gratitude abound.

Never forget, God's able and He will never fail.

Celebrate every victory – big or small — let joy prevail.

Enjoy where you are on the way to where you're going.

God's balance is what keeps His peace
and blessings always flowing.

Be Encouraged

You may think no one notices
the good things that you do.
You think no one will understand
the trials that you go through.
You think you can't be lifted up
because of things you've done,
or feel you're in an endless race
that never can be won.
There is someone named Jesus
who is with you every day.
He knows your heart. He knows your past
and loves you anyway.
He'll never turn His back
whenever you don't do things right.
Keep praising Him and live a life
that's pleasing in His sight.
Through Him you will find strength, and joy,
and perfect peace indeed;
for He is love, and He is Lord, and
He is all you need!

Because You're There

Dear Lord, let me seek Your face and put You first today.

Let me put my trust in You and let You lead the way.

Please forgive my unbelief.

Please hear me when I pray.

Lord, I am reminded that You're with me every day.

Situations sew a cloth to make me doubt You're there.

Threads of circumstance try to unravel that You care.

Dark colors of chaos stitched in places that are bare, but

the Master's Holy Comforter is present everywhere.

Tests and trials can paint a scene

to make me think I'm lost.

A canvas of no value (some agreed) that should be tossed.

Brush strokes of confusion

with no pattern splashed across,

but the Master knew the true value

and so He paid the cost.

I can never thank You Lord,

for all You've done for me.

I know that there are

wondrous things You do that I can't see.

I know that You are on the throne still watching over me;

for if You weren't there, Father God,

I know I'd cease to be.

13

Begin and End with Praise

There are no more instructions
to start and end your days.
Just lift your eyes to heaven,
then begin and end with praise.
No idle conversation.
No flowery words will do.
Just begin and end with praise
because of what He's done for you.
Each day when you awaken
and open your eyes wide,
praise Him for grace and mercy.
Praise Him 'cause you're alive.
Each evening when you settle down
and close your eyes to rest,
whisper one more praise
because you're covered and
you're blessed.
There are no more instructions
to start and end your days.
Just lift your eyes to heaven,
then begin and end with praise.

Choices

Life is filled with many things
you can't control, that's true.
If you want to change your fate,
here's what you can do:
Try letting go of yesterday
(don't live in the past).
Stop wasting time on negative things
(the days go by too fast).
Stop wishing for what used to be
(enjoy today instead).
Don't be afraid to take a risk,
or fear what lies ahead.
Each sunrise brings another chance
to start life fresh and new.
Each day is what you make it.
Now, the choice
is up to you!

Connection

No matter what happens in my life,

I cannot make it alone.

I recognize fully the things that I do

are not done on my own.

I'm part of something much greater

that only God could plan.

He made me special. He made me unique.

I'm fashioned by His own hand.

He did not make me to stand alone.

Part of the Master's design

was to give me a chance to touch someone's life,

and allow their life to touch mine.

We need one another.

That's for sure a point we should never forget.

If we always treat others

the way that we should,

in our lives there will be no regret.

Remember that you're not an island.

There's much that life holds for you.

Embrace your connection with others

and see just what God will do.

Don't Complain

Here's your challenge for today, watch everything you say;

be determined not to utter one complaining word today.

Don't complain about co-workers.

Don't complain about your boss.

Don't complain about the job you have,

or the other job you lost.

Don't complain about your children.

Don't complain about your spouse.

Don't complain

about the things you need to fix around the house.

Don't complain about the borrowed things

'cause you don't have your own.

Don't complain

about the bill collectors calling on the phone.

Don't complain

because your clothes may be a little out of style.

Don't complain

when it's suggested you should go the extra mile.

Don't complain

because your meal has not been seasoned to your taste.

Don't complain

about the driver who just stole your parking space.

Even if your money's tight, or you've got aches and pains,

whatever state you find yourself the point is

don't complain.

Every time you mumble

when things aren't the way you'd choose,

there's someone thinking

they'd be blessed, if they were in your shoes.

God always has a reason.

He holds you in His hand.

Trust Him in your circumstance.

He always has a plan.

He knows the storms you're facing.

He will bring you through.

Never fail to praise Him.

That's what He expects from you.

Every time you're tempted to grumble just exclaim,

"I'm grateful for my present state.

I will not complain!"

Don't Wait

Don't wait. Don't procrastinate.
There's something you must do.
I can't tell you what it is.
The assignment is for you.
Perhaps a visit should be made,
send a note, mail a card.
A short "hello" by telephone
wouldn't really be very hard.
There's something that's been on your mind,
something you meant to start.
There's a reason why, whatever it is,
has been placed upon your heart.
Don't wait. Don't procrastinate.
Keep your focus and follow-through.
Someone else's assignment
may not be complete
until they've connected with you.

Dry Season

If you live long enough, you will face dry seasons in your life. It happens to everyone. No matter what you do, your labor just doesn't seem to be producing any fruit. You might even think things are getting worse rather than better. The dry seasons will usually produce two things: doubt and discouragement. Will I have enough? Can I do enough? Will there be enough… enough time, enough resources, enough money, enough strength, enough patience, enough… "Enough" seems to be the root of it all, and you can fill in the blanks any way you choose. Did you know it's possible to grow, even in a dry season? God is still God! He is a God of more than enough, even in your dry seasons. You will never "run out…" because He will never run out. There will always "be…" because He will always be. Concentrate on watering the seeds you have planted with your faith and trust God. He will be everything you need, even in a dry season, and you will reap a harvest. Believe me, you will!

Extra Strength

Every time God blesses me to greet another day,

I think about His "whispers," and what He'd like to say.

Today I think I've penned it right.

A few short lines for you

in case you need some extra strength

and if you're goin' through.

Have faith that God the Father will do just what He said.

Build your hope upon the Rock and

every Word you've read.

Remember God loved you so much

He sacrificed His Son.

God's love is unconditional in spite of things you've done.

He's greater than your problems.

He'll never let you down.

He's with you in a crowd,

or when there's no one else around.

Believe in Him no matter what.

Trust Him in all you do.

Be steadfast and His promises

will manifest for you.

Favor

By the power of the Holy Spirit

and the authority of the Word of God,

I declare and decree

the favor of God rests upon my life

because I have:

Faith, the substance of things hoped for and the evidence of things not seen. I know that God is able and His

Abundance exceeds all I can ask or think. I live a life of joy, a life of strength, and a life of prosperity. I live my life knowing I have

Victory on every level. My confidence is in God, and God alone. I am submitted to His will. I am committed to His way. I walk in

Obedience to His Word. My delight is in the Lord. He is my hope, my help, my protector, my provider… my everything. I can

Rest knowing that God has given me mercy and granted me grace. I rest knowing that the God of all glory lovingly rules and reigns in my life.

Yes, I have the favor of the Lord, and I will bless
Him and give Him praise forever and ever and ever…
Amen

For the Mountain

God, I thank You for every one of life's mountains.

With every climb, I grow stronger.

With every step, I grasp a new level toward my destiny.

Whenever I slip, it lets me know there is slack somewhere

and I hold even tighter to my rope of faith.

I learn not to look down.

Whenever I do, I waiver and

I must never take my eyes off the prize of the high calling.

God, I thank You.

Every mountain reminds me

I don't have to make the climb alone.

You are there to pull me up higher;

to catch me when I begin to fall;

to guide me when I begin to go off course

and take the long way 'round.

You are there to support me when I need to be still

and regain my strength.

Thank You for letting me know every mountain in my life

is just a stepping stone to something greater

which will be used for Your glory.

I would never have made it this far

had it not been for the mountains.

I would never have made it this far

had it not been for You.

In the midst of the climb today Lord,

I give you praise, and honor, and glory

for the mountain.

Freedom

Have you ever met people, no matter what,

the good is all they can find?

It has nothing to do with the things they've acquired.

They've learned how to free their mind.

They're no better or worse than anyone else.

They have ups and downs all the time.

They're just not consumed by the cares of this world

since they know how to free their mind.

You may have experienced a difficult life

with a past that is best left behind.

It doesn't matter what happened before

as long as you free your mind.

There are many prisons,

some with walls, some without.

There's confinement of every kind.

You can be free of what's keeping you bound

if you remember to free your mind.

Bound by old sentiments?

Bound by fear?

Bound by relationships too?

Are you bound by old habits?

Bound by opinions that others expressed about you?

Whatever you are, whatever you've done,

whatever you think you might be,

you'd be amazed at how much can be changed

as soon as you get your mind free.

Start seeing yourself as God sees you,

for you are His intended design.

He's faithfully holding you…

shaping you…

molding you…

surrender, and free your mind.

Getting God's Instructions

Father, at this moment
I don't have much to say.
I just want to know
what You would have me do today.
Thank You for being with me
and whispering in my ear.
Let me not lose a single Word,
give me new ears to hear.
Whatever my assignment
my heart, Oh Lord, please fill.
Then give me Your instructions
so that I may do Your will.

Give God the Glory!

In times that are unsettling

and you're not sure what to do,

take heart and be at peace,

because the Lord has plans for you.

Nothing can separate you from His purpose and His will,

if you would simply seek His face and learn how to be still.

When life seems so confusing, take time to hear His voice.

He desires the best for you, but you must make a choice.

Choose to trust a mighty God who'll never let you down.

All that you will ever need,

in Him it can be found.

Don't try to rush ahead of Him or drag and lag behind.

He knows just what He's doing

and He's always right on time.

You may not know the outcome

or where you should begin.

Where there's God there's always hope

and an expected end.

Be filled with expectation. God's in complete control.

Give Him all the glory,

then watch His plan unfold!!

Grow in God

As believers, we often speak about wanting the will of God; desiring to draw closer to Him; wanting to experience all that God has for us. We say we want to hear His voice and follow His direction. We say we want to go with God. Too often we fail to remember to "go with God" means we must also "grow in God." Once we give our lives to Him, He takes us step by step as little children to help us mature, just as any loving parent would. In raising our children, when they stumble and fall we pick them up, brush them off, let them know the hurt won't kill them and it's going to be all right. We encourage them to try again. As much as we want to give them everything they want, we still have to discipline them by not always letting them have their way. Sometimes, when they ask the same question over and over, and we feel they should already know the answer, we won't respond at all. We do these things to help them reach a level of maturity. God does the same with us. The stumbles and falls in life; hurts and disappointments; tests of trust in Him; seasons of delay; and times of silence are situations designed to help us mature in God. They are circumstances designed for us to reach a level in our relationship with Him where we KNOW He is our everything. We know we WILL experience every promise He has made, just as He intended. Worship Him. Praise Him. Seek His face. Study His Word. Listen in prayer and purpose each day to take another step to grow in God.

Half Way? No Way!

For those who profess to love the Lord and have a relationship with Him, hopefully you would agree that God is one hundred percent God, all by Himself. He is everything. He has, and is, the answer to all questions. He is Alpha and Omega; the beginning and the end; the first and the last. There is nothing that God begins that He doesn't complete. His Word does not return to Him void. He is faithful and when it comes to blessing His children, He is a "no-holds barred," supernatural, going-beyond-anything-you-could-ask-or-think, protecting, providing, loving, GOD! He goes all out for His children. If you are His, you can expect Him to bring you into your purpose and your destiny. What's more He is always, ALWAYS available to you. So, what would make you think you could be half-way with an all-the-way God?

He wants you to turn away from those things that are not like Him and walk in the path He has set. Will we just plain "blow it" from time to time? Surely we will. However, when we do, we can't be comfortable. We must sincerely go before Him with a repentant heart, being determined to change. We can't flirt with sin and feel that it's OK. Wherever you are right now, God wants more for you, but you must choose. Ask yourself, "Does the world even recognize that I belong to Him?" Begin there and really search your heart. You can't live half-way for an all-the-way God.

Think about it today. If you're not where you want to be, if you're not where you need to be, it's time to make some decisions.

Heart Song

Father, as I start my day, You order my steps

and guide my way.

I just feel compelled to say, "Lord, I love You."

For everything You've done for me, especially things

I could not see, I just know I have to be… close to You.

I feel Your strength at every turn.

You give me grace I did not earn.

There's so much more I want to learn… about You.

Father God, don't take Your peace.

I find in You a sweet release.

I need You more. I beg you please… don't leave me.

I give You praise and honor too.

The glory all belongs to You.

I'll do whatever You want me to do… gladly.

When I've tried with all my might,

I know I'm precious in Your

sight 'cause You still love me, wrong or right… amazing.

I'll worship You and give You praise.

That's how I'll start and end my days,

I'll sing this short, sweet, heartfelt phrase,

"Lord, I love You!"

He's Right There

If God came in the flesh today

to spend some time with you,

what kinds of things would you say to Him?

What kinds of things would you do?

Would your conversation be the same

as it is from day-to-day,

or would you have to refrain from the kind of things

you would usually say?

Would you conduct yourself differently?

Would you be at ease?

When you review your daily routine

do you think God would be very pleased?

When you turn on your favorite TV show,

or stop to read a book,

would you want to share those things with Him?

Would you want Him to take a look?

Too often we think of the Father as being so far away,

but the truth is

He's right there by your side each and every day.

He's your friend and your constant companion.

He sees and knows all that you do.

As you go through your day just remember,

He's right there to spend time with you.

Just because I'm HIS

In the still of the early morning hours,
when all is quiet around me
I slowly open my eyes,
draw in a long deep breath and smile.
I am grateful to be alive.
He has chosen to keep me safe through another night;
allowed me to awake to another day that He has made;
just because He loves me and
just because I am His.
Today is a day to reflect upon His goodness and His grace.
Today I will take time to worship Him
because of who He is
and thank him for all the things He has done for me,
just because I am His.
For every struggle and every trial;
for things that were
overwhelming for me to handle on my own;
for every trouble imaginable that I have faced…
He has stood beside me,
walked with me, carried me, and cared for me,
just because I am His.
When people I've loved have left me;
when those in whom I put my trust betrayed me;

when no one seemed to understand

my hurts and I felt empty and isolated;

I talked to Him.

He listened.

He comforted me and let me know

that I am never alone,

because I am His

When I was faced with bills I couldn't pay;

debts I thought were insurmountable;

threats of foreclosure and repossessions;

notices of evictions and interrupted service;

He always, always, always gave me grace to go through;

showed me unmerited favor;

made a way out where I thought there was no way;

and He did it all,

just because I am His

When I was very ill;

when I could hardly take another breath because of pain;

when doctors' reports delivered nothing but bad news;

He took away the pain;

confounded the physicians;

and I am whole and healed today,

because I'm His.

When I abused myself with addictions trying to escape;

when I surrounded myself with people

and things that were

destructive and then felt so ashamed…

He picked me up;

cleaned me up;

and gave me another chance;

just because I am His.

When I wonder why He never left me;

why He forgives me still;

why He's so faithful to me;

why He gave His only begotten Son

that whosoever believed on him would not perish

but have ever lasting life; He reminds me softly,

it's because I am His.

He has shown me if I delight in Him

and walk along the path

that He has chosen for me,

He will bless me beyond measure,

because I am His.

If I trust Him, depend on Him, seek Him first,

and give Him what belongs to Him,

He will always provide for me,

because I am His.

When the world says I am not good enough,

I remember that

I am His creation. He designed me just the way I am

and I am fearfully and wonderfully made.

I can celebrate who and what I am,

because I am His.

I will praise Him, and I will worship Him,

and He will go to war for

me, and no weapon formed against me shall prosper,

because I am His.

And now, at the close of the day as I lie in bed,

and all is still around me,

I draw in a long deep breath and smile.

I am grateful to be alive.

He chose to keep me safe throughout another day;

showed me how to be a blessing to someone else;

allowed me to fulfill another part of my destiny…

Why?

Just because he loves me

and just because I'm His.

Hold On

When fighting all the trials of life
with problems everywhere,
you pray, and wait, and praise Him,
yet the answers just aren't there.
Don't be discouraged or give up.
The battle is fought and won.
God loves you so very much
He sacrificed His son.
No matter what you're going through,
hold on and have no doubt.
God's power, His grace and mercy and
YOUR FAITH
will bring you out.

I Believe for You

I believe the best for you today.
I believe God has something planned
for your life
that only He can do,
and it will come to pass.
I believe that someone you love
will come to have a personal relationship
with God.
I believe you will begin
to fellowship with God
on a higher level.
I believe that a prayer
you've prayed many times
will be answered.
I believe a dream you've put on the shelf
will begin to stir within you once again,
and this time the outcome will be
so much greater than you anticipated,
you will praise Him for the delay
as well as the victory.
I believe in the awesome power
of a mighty God.
I believe He is opening doors so wide

you will know the blessing

that's been chasing you

has caught you at last.

I believe in healing for you;

and miracles for you;

and prosperity for you;

and wisdom for you;

and unconditional love for you.

I believe God will give everything

you will ever need

to weather every storm,

and give you strength for every battle.

I believe He will bless you exceeding abundantly,

because I believe God can do anything!

Nothing…nothing…nothing is too hard for Him!

He's proven Himself so faithful to me,

I believe He will come through for you.

I believe in God's very best for you today.

Won't you believe it too?

Whatever it is, begin to say, "God, I believe …"

and see what He will do just for you!

I Rejoice Today

Father, I rejoice today!

There may be many things in my life

that are not what I expected,

or not what I would have foreseen,

but I rejoice today!

When I think of how faithful You have been to me,

my heart overflows with love for You.

Were it not for Your grace,

I don't know where I would be today.

So many wrong choices;

so many decisions made without Your guidance;

so many slips;

but You have continued to hold me

in the palm of your hand

and bless me time and time again.

Thank You

for all the times You did not allow me to have my way.

Thank You

for the requests You put on hold

until Your perfect timing created just the right atmosphere

for Your miracles to unfold.

Thank You

for removing things from my life

when I didn't understand why they had to be removed.

Thank You

for giving me strength and peace

to release those things that would have kept me bound

and delayed my destiny.

Thank You

for giving me strength and wisdom

to trust You above all else and believe Your Word.

I am so grateful that You continue to forgive me

for all the things I do that are not pleasing in Your sight.

Thank You

for mercies that are new every morning.

If it had not been for You being on my side,

I can't imagine…

I just can't imagine…

God, I rejoice today

for You are my Savior and my Lord!

You are a mighty God and You deserve all my praise,

forever… and ever… and ever…

In the Twinkling of an Eye

Dedicated to Trecolia Bussey who believed God rather than the stroke that attempted to derail His purpose and plans for her life. She requested a poem about her experience, and God gave me the words to grant her request. Through her strength and courage, He reminds us of our frailty and our triumph.

In the twinkling of an eye or the waving of your hand,

that's how quickly things can turn

from what appears to be life's plan.

Everything seems all mapped out.

The path ahead quite clear.

Pressing toward the mark.

Reaching new heights year to year.

Even in the struggles there are feelings of control

knowing hard times won't last always.

You can reach another goal.

Everything in order. Life neatly arranged.

Then in the twinkling of an eye, everything has changed.

Something unexpected. Something never planned.

All at once you're overwhelmed.

You've been dealt an unfair hand.

That is where I found myself one day a short while back.

My world had been turned upside down.

Nothing was intact.

It can't be fixed. It can't be changed.

Life will never be the same, but

in the midst of everything I called upon His name.

I activated all my faith, relying on His Word,

refusing to believe reports and negatives I'd heard.

My God is a healer and one thing I understood,

in the twinkling of an eye He can turn the bad to good.

He is my Provider, My Lord and Shepherd too.

Just as He has touched my life,

He'll do the same for you.

I'm walking down a new path now.

I'm standing strong and tall.

I'm submitted to an awesome God

who sees and knows it all.

In the twinkling of an eye, I might have ceased to be.

Instead God had a different plan and He's still using me.

Whatever state you find yourself,

there's something you must do.

Keep your faith and trust in God for He has plans for you.

If you're on the mountaintop,

or think life's passed you by,

know God's still God and He can move

in the twinkling of an eye.

It's All in the Name

Not for form or fashion or what I hope to gain,

just because I love Him, I'll call upon His name.

I know there's power in the name

'cause chains begin to break.

The very sound of *Jesus'* name will make a demon shake.

At the name of *Jesus*, I know every knee shall bow

and every tongue confess He's Lord;

not only then, but now.

When I feel I can't take any more –

and I do from time to time --

I whisper the name of *Jesus*

to gain strength and a renewed mind.

Oh, the name of *Jesus*, when soft and sweet I call,

He knows I've given up my will and I've surrendered all.

Have you ever tried it (morning, night or noon)…

just said the name of *Jesus*

'till His presence filled the room?

You will feel your burdens lifted.

You'll feel a sweet release.

It only happens when He comes

and wraps you up in peace.

If you don't know where to turn

and you don't know what to do,

say the name of *Jesus*, and let Him take you through.

Say the name because He's worthy. Let it be understood,

sometimes you want to say His name

just because He's good.

Not for form or fashion or what you hope to gain,

just because you love Him, right now,

stop… and say His name.

J E S U S

As I behold the beauty that surrounds me,
I am reminded that the

Joy of the Lord is my strength, and His strength is made perfect in my weakness. Every day I wake up with the

Expectation and anticipation that God can and will do exactly what He said according to His Word. I will

Serve Him with gladness as I enter into His gates with thanksgiving and into His courts with praise. I now

Understand who He is and who I am in Him. I have experienced the greatest miracle of all

Salvation.

As long as I have Jesus, I have everything I need.

Joined

It's said, "no man is an island,"

and this I know is true.

In some way you have need of me.

For sure, I've need of you.

God wanted all His children

fitly joined you see --

to be the church, the body --

to be His family.

God gave each one a certain gift

and through the Word we know

as each part does its special work,

it helps us all to grow.

Lord, thank You for your wisdom

and guidance every day,

so we might hold to truth in love

like You in every way.

Let Me Be A Blessing

Good Morning, Heavenly Father!
Show me someone to bless today.
Let me take my mind off myself
when I begin to pray.
Let me uplift my co-workers,
or ask You to answer a prayer
for a neighbor who's been struggling,
who needs to know You're there.
Please keep our soldiers protected
and bless those left at home.
Let me send someone a message
to let them know they're not alone.
Master, draw a couple close today
who may have grown apart.
Help them rekindle
all the love that once was in each heart.
Let me embrace the children
and show them lots of love.
Building positive self-esteem
can start with just one hug.
Give me a kind word for a stranger
and encouragement for a friend.
Let me tell someone to trust in You

whatever state they're in.

Father, thank You for every assignment

and every opportunity

so that I can be a blessing today

as I share the Christ in me.

Little Things

Sometimes it's the little things
that make or break your day,
like the kind word you might give someone
you meet along the way.
The little extra time you take
to show love to a child,
or when you slow your pace
to greet a stranger with a smile.
The simple words like "thank you"
don't take too long to say and
they make a world of difference in someone else's day.
Have a little patience;
put yourself in someone's place;
show them a little mercy;
give them a little grace.
Don't always be so quick to judge based on what you see.
Things are hardly ever what they first appear to be.
Many little acts of love can easily be found,
if you slow down just a second and take a look around.
Don't be in a hurry and be careful what you say.
Remember, it's the little things
that make or break your day.

Love Note

Father, there are times I just want to be in Your presence and tell You that I love You. That's all I want to do. No requests, no petitions, no hidden agendas, I just want to allow myself to be close to You. When I think of where I could have been, then I think of all You've done for me, I just want to take a moment and tell you how very grateful I am. As mighty as You are, You still have enough love and patience to continue fixing me up and cleaning me up for Your use. God, how I adore You. You are indeed altogether lovely and I exalt You. I only have myself to give, and with all my faults and flaws that doesn't seem like very much, but I know little becomes much when it's placed in Your hands. When there was no one to comfort me when I needed it, or hear my cries in the dead of night, You were always there, always so faithful. Thank You for holding me; for wanting the best for me; for not rejecting me, even when I rejected you; for covering me under the blood of Your precious Son; for letting me know I am never alone. Evidence of You is all around me, in every cloud, every leaf, every blade of grass, every drop of rain, all You, Lord… all You. Father, if You never do another thing for me, I'm so blessed to be Your child. All I desire is to please You. I want to worship You and praise You until all the noise of life is silent. When You whisper in our quiet time, I know You are my everything and I am overjoyed!

Men of God

Men are often identified by their name, their title, or their prowess in one field of endeavor or another, but men of God are acknowledged because they embody characteristics that transcend recognition of their strength, physique, or intellect. They must first be known by their submission to an awesome, omnipotent God. Men of God quickly realize in order to rule, they must first be able to serve and serve with gladness. While they can stand strong against storms and struggles, they also know how to fall on their knees, unashamed, and worship their way through. They are men of vision and men of purpose. They are role models of integrity who are not caught in compromise; loving men who treat the women in their lives as God's gifts; and men of character who are excellent leaders, as well as faithful followers. When I look around, I see men who are not afraid to be set apart. I see men who play both roles as parents. I see men who are courageous and sensitive at the same time. I hear the hearty laughter of a father delighting in his children and the tongue of a prayer warrior covering his family. I look around and see men who know who they are, and are clear on whose they are as well. When I look at you, I see a man of valor who sets the standard high exemplifying these characteristics. I look at you and see a man who can stand with boldness and declare, "I am a man of destiny for I am a man of God!"

Ministry

Are you doing the will of the Father

who placed you in the earth?

The Creator, who knew how He would use you

even before your birth,

has chosen you for a purpose.

You've been ordained for your task

and if you do what's required of you,

He'll give you whatever you ask.

You should go and bring forth fruit, fruit that will remain.

Then whatever you ask of the Father,

be sure to ask in Jesus' name.

Remember, you are not your own.

You're here by His design

to serve in the work assigned to you.

He chose you for this time.

Since He has work for you to do,

He'll give you what you need, but

you must plow and you must plant.

There's work to sowing seed.

Take joy in all your assignments.

Love others as God has loved you.

Then you will fulfill your purpose

and receive all God's intended for you.

Mirror, Mirror

When I look in the mirror, what do I see?
What has been formed in the reflection called me?
Can anyone see all the hurt and the pain?
Can anyone see the scars I've obtained?
Can anyone see the years of mistrust,
the hatred, jealousy, envy and lust?

When I look in the mirror, what do I see?
What's hidden behind the reflection called me?
Have I managed somehow to put on a show
so others who're watching the mirror won't know
it's all just a front, a charade, just a game
that's been played with precision disguising the shame?

There does come a time when you tire of deception.
You're weary of things that don't make a connection
with good things that you feel lie dormant inside.
The treasure that evil has tried hard to hide.

And then someone tells you
(they just plant a seed)
about an Almighty God
who has just what you need.

They talk of the Father,

and Jesus the Son,

and the Holy Spirit,

ah yes, three in one.

They talk of a God who knows you inside out.

A God who can tell you what you're all about.

They tell you He loves you with your imperfection.

He's right there to guide you and give you direction.

He's God. He won't leave you.

He'll stay by your side.

He let His Son die so that you can abide.

When I look in the mirror, what do I see?

Is the change of God's love now reflecting from me?

Does the mirror now show that I've been reborn

and through the Almighty my life's been transformed?

Does the mirror now show that my past is erased

and the favor of God has taken its place?

When I look in the mirror now,

what do I see?

A new creature in Christ,

that's the image of me!

My Word

A Word can be a single thought.

A Word can be a phrase.

A Word can be remembrances that send you into praise.

Sometimes you hear a Word and think

the revelation's missed, but it's lingered in your spirit man

for such a time as this.

A Word can be your anchor, or your lifeline to hold on.

A Word can be your answer

when you think all hope is gone.

A Word, one Word, is all it takes

and when it comes to mind,

you'll find yourself with renewed strength

and power every time.

Do you know what your Word is,

that the Word God speaks to you,

that it lets you know He's got your back

and you can make it through?

Father, as I worship You and I take time to pray,

speak Lord, because I know I'll need

my Word

from You today!

No Matter What...

One of the enemy's most effective tactics to stop you in your tracks is a threat. Many times nothing actually happens. It doesn't have to. You will self-destruct based on what you think might happen. Bullies will instill terror in a child at school by just telling them, "I'll see you when the bell rings." Your boss says, "One more incident and you're fired." The bill collectors call and threaten to repossess your car, foreclose on your home, ruin your credit, etc., if you don't pay right now. Your spouse threatens to leave you. What will you do? How will you survive? What about the children? Some of the threats may become reality, but no matter what, you still have a God!

Threats are a doorway to fear. Slam the door and lock it. Lock it with your faith. You may not have what you need to handle everything, but you have a God who can do anything. If the bully shows up; if you lose your possessions; if your job lets you go; if your "boo" leaves; God will pick you up, dust you off, and give you greater. He can do it because nothing is too hard for Him!

No matter what is threatening you today, let your self-talk take over and declare, "I have a God and He is well able…" Say it again, "I have a God and He is well able." Say it with power… Say it with conviction… Say it with faith, "I have a God and He is well able, no matter what!"

Passing Through

Wading through a growing list of all I had to do,

suddenly I heard a whisper,

"You're just passing through.

The things you do are temporal.

They are not meant to last.

You're spending time on meaningless things

and time goes by too fast.

Whether mountaintop experience,

or day you must face strife,

they're all planned in preparation

for your eternal life."

All at once I shifted focus

and changed my point of view,

as I remembered this is not my home,

I'm just passing through.

Peace

I find there is no greater peace
when I take time to pray,
than knowing I can lay "it" down
and I can walk away.
"It" may be all my problems.
"It" may be thoughts of lack.
"It" may be insecurities
when my thinking gets off track.
I'll only pick up faith and hope.
I'll only pick up love.
I'll only keep the things that
God has given from above.
I need not wrestle, fret, or fear.
I'll trust Him when I pray.
Whatever "it" is,
I'll lay "it" down,
and let God have His way.

Personal Prayer

Good Morning, Heavenly Father. I come to You today

grateful for another chance to bow my head and pray.

I want to tell You thank You

for keeping me through the night.

I know as long as I trust in You everything will be alright.

Thank You for the children and Godly parents too,

who'll train them up to know Your Word and

give themselves to You.

Thank You for the soldiers who're fighting far away,

who sacrifice so we can enjoy

the freedom we have today.

Thank You for those in authority.

Let them know Your grace.

Give them Godly wisdom and let them seek Your face.

Thank You for the time

that You have graciously granted me.

Don't let me waste a moment, Lord, or spend it selfishly.

There're so many things to thank You for,

like joy, and peace, and rest.

So many people who need to know,

through You they can be blessed.

I'm reminded I'm on assignment

that's really not about me.

I'm chosen to let Your light so shine

that someone else can see

they don't have to be in darkness.

They can come out of sin.

They can be loved and forgiven,

if they would let You enter in.

Let me be about Your business Lord,

and as I continue to pray

give me instruction so I can be sure

to fulfill my assignment today.

Play it Again

Have you ever had a restless night? I do from time to time.

Then I wake up overwhelmed

with "stuff" that's on my mind.

Old, left over problems that I have yet to solve.

Unpleasant situations in which I had to be involved.

Failures, disappointments, faults all crowded in my head.

Misinterpretation of things I'd heard or things I'd said.

That's when I have to tell my flesh,

"This is not the way

I intend to start my morning, or go about my day.

Yesterday was yesterday. Today, I start brand new.

Giving "air time" to the enemy is one thing I will not do."

Instead of hitting rewind

to the track of "things gone wrong,"

I decide to push fast forward till I find a "triumph" song.

Melodies of mercy, how forgiving God can be,

harmonies of all the times He's shown His love to me.

God takes notes of confusion pounding in my ear

and turns them into quiet chords playing soft and clear.

Whenever I need His refrain to replay as it should,

I let gratitude take over and I focus on the good.

If you happen to wake up with clutter on your mind,

let God orchestrate your day and things will work out fine.

Power

You know that you have power
over what you think and say.
When you exercise that power
you can then affect your day.
Since you've surrendered everything to God
you can be bold.
Your thoughts and conversation
are now under His control.
If you say, "Today's victorious,"
and in all things see the good,
you will have a day of victory
just like you said you would.
If there's confusion all around you
and you start speaking peace,
the atmosphere will change
and all the chaos will soon cease.
You can mumble,
you can grumble over issues from your past.
You can build a bridge, get over it,
and move on with life at last.
You can talk about old hurts
until they're open wounds again.

You can allow God's love to heal you
and let broken places mend.
You have power to choose life over death;
faith instead of fear;
have strength instead of weakness;
hope rather than despair.
Speak the Word; trust and obey;
let Christ's mind be in you;
and you will see real power
as God works through all you do.

Praise Break

If you opened up your eyes
that means God kept you through the night. Praise Him
for there's one more chance to see the wrong made right.
If you have a mind to serve Him
because He's shown you grace,
you have a mind to praise Him anytime and anyplace.
When you know Him
as provider, Shepherd, Lord and King
you can praise Him as a God
who is in charge of everything.
You may not have the "things" you want
or think you need right now.
Be grateful for the things you have
and praise Him anyhow.
Even if you're unemployed
and things aren't going your way,
still praise Him 'cause a million folks
didn't even wake up today.
Don't be tricked into complaining.
Don't focus on what's not.
Stand still, throw your head back,
and praise God on the spot.
If you know about His goodness

and all the things He's done,

you know the battle is not yours.

It has been fought and won.

Praise Him because He's worthy.

Praise Him all your days.

Don't explain it.

Don't contain it.

It's just time to give God praise.

Proceed

Father, I wonder where we would be

if we followed Your Word explicitly.

If we studied the scriptures to be more like You,

then actually did what You've told us to do.

Your Word is quite clear on what's wrong and what's right.

There's no in between. There is darkness or light.

We've been called as believers to be set apart

in our thoughts, in our actions, with what's in our heart.

We can't "church" once a week and then feel at ease

to live our lives six days just as we please.

We can't expect favor, and that which is good

without doing what You have told us we should.

The end is near.

We can waste no more time.

There are souls to be saved.

There are lives on the line.

It must be evident that we are Yours

without Bible in hand or a sweet, "Praise the Lord."

We must carry ourselves so the world will know

we are children of God wherever we go.

Father, I pray that I won't compromise.

I will look in the mirror and open my eyes.

Then I'll ask you to change whatever's in me

that might cause me to miss what you want me to be --

an example to draw someone closer to You

by doing the things You require me to do.

Quiet

Sound is sometimes deafening.

Sometimes it is sweet.

At times I find my inner voice and outer sounds compete.

The sounds of life are everywhere no matter where I go.

Traffic, conversation, even howling winds that blow

can sound like so much jumbled noise ringing in my ear.

I want to turn the volume down and let my thinking clear.

Every now and then I know

I need a quiet place

where I can sit, reflect a bit, and then re-set my pace.

"God, I need that quiet time where just the two of us

can get together one-on-one, no clamor and no fuss.

With a flurry of activity and many tasks to do.

I really want a quiet place to sit and talk with You.

It might not take an hour. A brief moment will be fine.

I just need peace and quiet to let You renew my mind."

If you ever feel the sounds of life

are more than you can take,

find yourself a quiet place, catch a little break

and focus on the Father. Now hush, don't make a sound.

Give yourself some quiet time and turn your day around.

Reflections

On a cold and dreary day as I sat alone to pray,

I wondered how "this" and "that" had come to be.

Then I raised my hands in praise,

while thinking of the days

God had stepped into my life and rescued me.

All at once in my small space

just like a warm embrace,

I could feel His loving presence fill the room.

That quickly put a stop to the devil's evil plot

to fill my day with doubt, and doom, and gloom.

Now, your "this" may not be mine

and your "that" may be a time

when you simply didn't know what you would do.

Things might have looked quite bleak.

You may have thought you'd faced defeat, but

God showed up and helped you make it through.

Take a little time

to reflect and free your mind

of all the things you think are facing you.

Worship God above

and allow the Father's love

to do what only Father God can do.

Relationship

This morning I was thinking, in my private time,

how often we say, "Father, I am Yours and You are mine."

Yet many times we overlook the things that we must do

when we say, "Lord, I want a real relationship with You."

For instance, do I seek God's face before I seek His hand?

That's one of His instructions and part of His daily plan.

Do I treat my body like the temple that it is

and not do things that contradict the fact that I am His?

Am I asking for a pure heart, or for clean hands to raise

as I enter into His gates with thanks

and into His courts with praise?

Am I praying without ceasing

day-by-day and week-by-week,

before I realize

I didn't give God time to speak?

And before I even dare to ask the smallest thing of God,

do I take the time to worship Him?

Worship isn't hard.

Help us, Father.

Show us where we've erred that we might be

what you want in order to be drawn closer to thee.

Lord, we ask forgiveness for the things we've failed to do.

Let nothing keep us from a real relationship with you.

Rest

It's easy to begin to stress with all that lies ahead.

We wonder how we'll manage

all the things we've come to dread.

We're buried in our daily lives

with work and bills and such;

and things we should have overcome

consume our time too much.

Out of our frustration we will often try to find

a way to change our circumstance,

depending on our mind.

Thanks be to God!

He whispers and assures us quietly

to keep our trust in Him alone

because He holds the key.

God shows us in the smallest ways

how truly great He is.

He shows He cares for everything,

for everything is His.

I began to count the many ways in which He never fails.

He showed me how He orchestrates minute, divine details.

As I wandered through the Garden,

God prompted me to see

there amid the blossoms

the smallest bumble bee.

Cradled in the petals, protected, unafraid,

this tiny creature rested in a bed that God had made.

I smiled and was reminded,

if God did this without a fuss,

how much He must provide and care for every one of us.

When you're feeling over burdened

and you will from time to time,

RELAX,

just like the bumble bee

REST

and ease your mind.

God will never leave you.

He holds you in His hand.

Whenever there's a trial,

there is a reason and a plan.

He's such an awesome Father.

He's kind and faithful too.

If He cares this much for the bumble bee,

think how He must love you.

Shadows

After hurried appointments and meetings –
a round of all work and no play --
I was anxious to get home, take time to relax,
and forget all about the day.

Looking forward to selfish unwinding
after rushing here and there,
I parked a short distance from my home
to walk and enjoy the night air.

I noticed these shadows as I walked along
the busy, dimly lit street;
shadows, forms, shapes and figures,
some rugged, some soft, all discreet.

Large shadows as I hurried past
and quickly looked away.
Small shadows that I tried to ignore
in case they had something to say.

There's a shadow bundled in the doorway;
another over there by the tree;
from another shadow a faded sign

with two printed words, "Help me."

Why don't these shadows disappear?
They're an irritant, an eyesore at best.
You would think they've decided to set up house
and make the street their address.

"Let me speak on behalf of the shadows."
I heard a voice strong and clear say,
"I have a few questions to ask of you
and there're a few things that you need to hear.
What happened to all your compassion?
When did you become so great?
Do you think because you are blessed today
you have a right to judge and berate?
A sudden shift in the timing of life,
a circumstance with more loss than gain,
and you could become just a shadow
battered by wind and rain;
or parched by the sun with no shelter or shade,
once hoping to get a new start.
Now, carrying all your possessions,
your whole life in a bag or a cart.
What you call shadows are real men and women,
each with a story to tell.

Oh, dear God, I ask your forgiveness.

What on earth has happened to me?

Have I become so consumed with myself

that I can no longer see?

As I stood there ashamed, softly crying,

I knew (just like I know my name)

from the moment I heard the voice of God

I would never see shadows the same.

Pause when you next see a shadow.

Take a good long look and you'll see

the shadows have well defined faces

of people just like you and me.

I'll never take what I have for granted.

I'll not look down on those I pass by.

That night God helped me remember

there, but for His grace, go I.

Someone is Watching You

How do I live when I think no one's looking?
What do I do, thinking no one can see?
Am I living my life by God's Word and instructions?
Am I the example He wants me to be?
Am I speaking His Words of healing and faith?
Do I encourage someone when they're down?
Do I carry myself in an ungodly way
when there's no other believer around?
Do I gossip about other people
and cloak it as knowledge for prayer?
Are carnal influences feeding my spirit
when nobody else is there?
I must be Christ-like in all that I do,
set apart so that others might see.
How I live when I think no one's watching
is the true test of Christ in me.

Steal Away

Good Morning, Heavenly Father.

Thank You for this day.

You saw fit to give me breath

and start me on my way.

While we have spoken briefly,

we haven't spent much time.

Many thoughts of tasks ahead seem to crowd my mind.

I suffer from busy-i-tis.

I feel I have so much to do.

I forget the only important things

are the things I do for You.

Forgive me for my negligence

when I set my priorities,

if I don't begin in worship

with bowed head and bended knees.

Father, You're so good to me.

You show Your love each day

when in the midst of all my mess,

You never turn away.

Father please, if You don't mind, I'd like to start anew.

Let me steal away

right now, today

and spend some time with You.

Talking to My Father

I awoke this morning with a smile upon my face.

I was aware of God's new mercies and His amazing grace.

I thought about His love

and how His Son had died for me.

I thought about the blood that Jesus shed on Calvary.

I know I have no time to waste.

There's no time to complain.

Since He has renewed my mind, I must not stay the same.

I must be Kingdom minded.

Worldly things I will not hold.

I must decrease and die to self, and let God take control.

Tears began to fill my eyes as I lay there very still,

and told my Father, "Use me Lord. Use me as You will.

I trust you Lord,

though there are things I do not understand.

I know You have a reason and I know You have a plan.

Create in me a clean heart and clean hands to lift in praise.

Lord, just let me worship You as I live out my days.

Get the glory from my life in everything I say and do.

I surrender Lord,

because I owe it all to You."

That's Why

Have you ever noticed when you sit down to pray,

a million things distract you,

getting in your way?

Have you tried to be obedient when God said,

"Read My Word,"

then found yourself so sleepy

that you doubted what you heard?

Ever stopped to tell a stranger something really nice

and they spoke harshly to you,

making you think twice?

Have you ever been determined to sow out of your need

and watched a crisis come along and gobble up your seed?

Did you ever ask the Father,

"Why is so much going wrong?"

and at that moment,

have Him place in you a worship song.

It's true His ways are not our ways.

His thoughts are His alone.

Yet we know for sure we're never,

ever "out here" all alone.

That's why we must surrender all to God and to His plan.

That's why we must keep holding on

to God's unchanging hand.

The "Cloak" of Christianity

Cloak: a loose outer garment; something that conceals; pretense or disguise

Many years ago, the fashion preference for outer wear was called a cloak. Unlike the form fitted buttoned down coats of today, a cloak could be comfortably draped around your shoulders. It was designed to fit loosely for ease and freedom of movement. Today it seems there are people in the body of Christ who treat their belief in God like an old fashioned cloak, freely putting it on when it's convenient, and quickly taking it off when it suits them. They wear their cloak in the church, at church functions, on church property, when they are with other professed believers... However, when they are out in the world -- where their witness is really important -- they easily slip out of their cloak of Christianity, preferring to dress in a cape of carnality instead. To be Christ-like is not something to be put-on or removed like a piece of clothing, depending on where you are, or with whom. It must be a part of you. The light and love of Christ must shine through you at home, at work, at the restaurant, in the drive-thru, at the grocery store, at the car wash, anywhere you are and everywhere you are. Check yourself today. What are you wearing: the cloak of Christianity, or the coat of Christ?

The Fight

Ever feel like you're in a prize fight,

being hit from every side?

You're being struck so hard you know you're blessed

just 'cause you've survived.

Right before you hit the mat and hear the count of "ten,"

something in you rises up and you stand to fight again.

This time you bob, and weave, and stick,

and counter every blow.

This time you're landing punches,

fighting with everything you know.

Jab – God is able. Uppercut – He cannot fail.

Combination – Grace and Mercy.

Right cross – God will prevail.

You're never in the ring alone.

In fact, remember this –

even though you fought this round,

the fight is already fixed.

Before the first bell signaled that the fight was to begin,

God had already given you

everything you'd need to win.

You're only in this fight because the enemy is mad.

He knows you're about to receive

the greatest blessing you've ever had.

So don't give in and don't give up.

You will win and there's no doubt.

God is in your corner and

He will surely bring you out.

The Menu

Will only natural food be consumed by you,

or will the Word of the Lord be on the menu?

Remember the saying, "you are what you eat?"

Then why not try eating a spiritual treat.

We can't fight the enemy with a holy force

if the things of the world have become our main course.

Looking for something to quench your thirst?

Did you consider 'living water' first?

You're feeling weak, but you know God is able.

Space has been reserved, just pull up to His table.

A full course meal sounds like a good plan, but

it must be nourishment to your Spirit man.

While balancing cholesterol and calories,

include His Word with your dietary needs.

When watching your weight as you think you should

oh taste and see

that the Lord is good!

The Power Within

Why is it some people seem to soar
while others think life is a horrible bore?
I believe it has something to do with the power within.
Some folks are all smiles, always upbeat.
There are some who stay down in despair and defeat.
The difference between them?
Their use of the power within.
We've all kinds of reasons to fail or succeed --
poverty, money, ambition or greed --
but which way do we channel the power that lies within?
It really isn't about your boss,
or piles of statements of profit and loss.
It's all about the power that lies within.
It's not always about the race
and whether or not you took first place;
on the way, did you discover the power within?
When the journey is undefined and
you don't want to waste precious time,
are you redirecting the power that lies within?
When the path at times is very unclear and
you're tempted to cry, or you're tempted to fear
are you guided instead by the power that lies within?
Who in your life plays a leading role?

Have you surrendered to man's control and
failed to tap into the limitless power within?
There is only one who defines you,
because He's the one who designed you.
He gave you all this power that lies within.
Don't cast it aside, or misuse it.
Don't leave it untouched, or abuse it.
Be careful how you handle the power within.
Treat it as though it's a rare precious gem
wrapped up in wisdom, placed there by Him
to help you stand through the storm,
that's the power within.
When doubters proclaim you can't make it,
and you don't even feel you can take it,
it's time to reach down and draw on the power within.
No one can predict all the turns you'll take;
when you will win or make a mistake; but
I know for sure everyone has a power within.
As long as you're willing to stay in the fight;
hold your head high
when you're wrong or you're right;
and refuse to give up before you even begin;
you can rise to the top and you'll never be stopped,
if you grab hold and use
the power you have within.

Think Good Thoughts

A very simple whisper, "think good thoughts today."

Don't dwell on any confusion

that might seem to block your way.

Think good thoughts about the person

you know has done you wrong.

Change your thoughts from hurt and anger

into a worship song.

If there is a situation that would

seem to pull you down,

think good thoughts about a mighty God

and watch things turn around.

Life's not always easy. At times it seems unfair,

but you know that God is able,

and you know that God is there.

Focus on the Father when defeat creeps in your mind.

Bring your thoughts into captivity. Don't waste any time

listening to the enemy and what he tries to say.

Cancel all the devil's plans.

Think good thoughts today.

Today by Request

According to the Word of the Lord

for all those who believe,

if you make a request of the Lord,

that request you shall receive.

I requested a day of victory, a day that was struggle free;

and my Heavenly Father, in His faithfulness

prepared no defeats for me.

I requested a day of blessings,

and that's exactly what I had.

God even made good things come

from things that were meant to be bad.

I requested a whole day – twenty-four hours –

when I could be without pain;

and because He's such an awesome God,

each day He granted the same.

I requested a day without bondage –

a day where I could be free.

He reminded me, that's why He sent his Son

to die on Calvary.

I requested a day in His presence.

His voice I wanted to hear.

I knew my requests had been granted

when He whispered in my ear,

"My child, these requests are no problem.
There's nothing that I wouldn't do,
if you will just worship and praise Me
I'm waiting to do them for you."
Today, my request is to love You, Lord
and draw nearer to You than before.
Let me do Your will, my life Lord please fill,
today and for evermore.

Watch Your Words

I was listening for a whisper. Instead I heard a scream.

'WATCH YOUR WORDS.
THEY'RE VERY POWERFUL.
SAY ONLY WHAT YOU MEAN.
YOU WILL HAVE THE WORDS YOU SPEAK.
BE CAREFUL WHAT YOU SAY.
THE ENEMY IS LISTENING
VERY CAREFULLY TODAY."

I don't know what lies ahead, or why there is a need
to be reminded of the power of words,
but words will plant a seed.
Be sure you're planting seeds of life
in things that you hold dear.
Do not put any negatives into the atmosphere.
If all the good God has for you is not coming your way,
perhaps it has something to do
with the kinds of things you say.
Speak healing when there's sickness.
Speak wealth without a dime.
Bring your thoughts into captivity
for you'll speak what's on your mind.

Watch your words. They're very powerful.

Be careful what you say.

Declare and decree the Word of the Lord

over everything each day.

We Will

Dear Heavenly Father, I thank You for this day You have given us to enjoy. We will indeed rejoice because we know as long as there is breath in our bodies, You still have something wonderful planned for us. We know that every stumbling block is a stepping stone to an even greater opportunity; therefore, we will never see a setback as failure. We will speak your Word over every situation because we know Your Words are swift and powerful. We will call upon the name of Jesus in our circumstance because we know demons flee at the mention of Your name. We will turn every critical thought of disappointment into one of life and love. We will turn every complaint into a statement of compassion. We will turn every doubt into a thought of determination to reach our destiny in You. We will pray relentlessly for the lost to come to know You, and ask You to bless our friends as well as our enemies. We will ask You to place a high hedge of protection around our families today, wherever they might be. We will look for ways to be of service to someone. And Father, in the midst of every thought, every task, every assignment, and every divine appointment, we will give You sacrifices of praise for You alone are worthy…Amen

What If…

What if God said that He was busy

and had other things to do

at a time when you were crying,

"Lord, please help me. I need You?"

What if God said, *"Not today. It's not a convenient time…"*

when you felt, without His help,

you would surely lose your mind?

What if God said, *"Sorry child, it's been a really hectic week.*

Try me a little later. Right now I think I'll sleep?"

That's not the kind of God we serve.

No matter what, He's there

to love and to protect us anytime and anywhere.

He sacrificed His only Son who dearly paid the cost

to make certain we were not alone

and no one would be lost.

Now, God has a request of us. He has one simple plea.

He's whispering to you right now, *"Just spend time with Me."*

If you take time to worship Him

and take some time to pray,

you will hear Him saying,

"Just spend time with Me today.
I have all the answers. I hold every key.
Take a moment to be still my child
and spend some time with Me."

When He Whispers

I love what He does

when He whispers in the morning.

I love what He does when I call upon His name.

I love what He does for me

just because He loves me.

I love what He does and that's why I can proclaim

He's my healer, my protector,

my deliverer and my king.

He's my shepherd, and my Savior,

and He's Lord of everything.

My provider, my redeemer,

the beginning and the end,

He's my help in time of trouble.

He's my Father. He's my friend.

Oh, I love what He does

when we spend our time together.

All I have, all I am, and all I ever hope to be

is because of what He does

when He whispers in the morning.

It's because of what He does

just for me.

Women of Excellence

We are young. We are single.

We are married. We are "seasoned."

We have a purpose and a destiny

to be women of excellence.

We are grandmothers and mothers; wives – sisters;

Grand-daughters – daughters.

we are striving to be …

we are proving to be…

we are teaching others to be…

women of excellence.

Whether we are at school -- in the workplace –

or in our homes;

classmates, family, co-workers, and friends --

those close to us -- and those we have not yet met --

will recognize the Christ in us by our words, actions,

and reactions

as we display the characteristics of

women of excellence.

We are all ages, colors, shapes, and sizes.

Each an original designed by God;

fashioned for His use for such a time as this;

to fulfill a divine plan; to do what only we can do as

women of excellence.

We are the essence of

Eve … Ruth … Esther … Deborah, … Sarah …

Mary … Miriam … Anna … Hannah,

with gifts and talents deposited IN us,

for a work that can only be done THROUGH us.

We are students, teachers, prophets,

preachers, homemakers,

risk takers, technicians, politicians,

praise leading and interceding.

We are a power source and a driving force.

We give honor to our Lord and Savior, Jesus Christ,

for He is first in our lives –

Alpha and Omega,

the beginning and the end,

the author and finisher of our faith --

and no weapon … no weapon … no weapon …

formed against us shall prosper, because

we are women of excellence!

You Matter

In the midst of your life's journey

as you stumble to find your way,

know that you matter.

If you don't feel you are important

To anyone else,

you are important to God and to His Kingdom.

You have to know that your life is not just about you.

You matter because someone else's life

will not be complete,

and their promises will not be fulfilled unless they hear the

resonance of your voice, or feel the strength in your hands.

You have been through more than most people

will ever be exposed to and you have survived!

You are the piece of the puzzle some people

have difficulty placing.

Your edges are not perfectly straight

There are no defined corners to help everyone

immediately see where you belong.

Even if you feel you've been tossed aside,

there will be an empty place

where you could have been -- should have been --

that no one else can fill.

It was meant specifically for you.

If you need a little encouragement today,

remember there is a purpose for you and you alone.

God loves you just that much.

You are important to Him.

You are important to the world.

Always remember,

you matter.

About the Author

Andrea L. Hines
*Mother, Grandmother, Author, Poet, Speaker,
Entrepreneur, Doctor of Divinity and Certified Life Coach*

This lady of many talents is a native of Washington, D.C. who currently resides in Raleigh, NC. Over the years, Andrea has performed in numerous community theatre and film projects; actively participated in literary associations; and narrated for the North Carolina Library for the Blind & Physically Handicapped and the Triangle Radio Reading Service. Her poetic work has been featured in local newspapers, national and international anthologies, and on Blue Mountain Arts greeting cards and products. It was in North Carolina where her relationship with God deepened and her creativity began to flow freely.

"I used to think God only spoke in a booming voice. I anticipated the earth would quake when He wanted to get my attention. You know, a "burning bush" experience. Instead, I find He loves to whisper to me in the quiet stillness of the early morning hours when it's just the two of us.

"Whether you are in a season of great success or a season of great struggle, you need to be encouraged from time to time.

"These specially selected verses from my time with Him are designed to speak to the heart and uplift the soul. Read them thoughtfully, cover to cover, or allow a title to catch your eye and ignite your curiosity. Either way, I pray you will allow His Words to touch you as only He can when He whispers!"

www.ingramcontent.com/pod-product-compliance
Lightning Source LLC
Chambersburg PA
CBHW060948050726

47592CB00003B/1147